Hodge

By the same author

Skevington's Daughter
The Player Queen's Wife
The Oslo Tram
Almost

Oliver Reynolds

Hodge

Areté Books

This collection was first published 2010 by Areté Books

An imprint of Areté Ltd

8 New College Lane, Oxford OX1 3BN

www.aretemagazine.com

ISBN 987-0-9562739-2-5

A CIP catalogue record for this book is available from the British Library.

Typeset and printed by the Information Press, Southfield Road, Eynsham, Oxford OX29 4JB.

The author thanks the Royal Literary Fund; Stephen Knight; and the editors of *Areté, Granta, Modern Poetry in Translation, New Welsh Review, Planet, Poetry Review, Poetry Wales* and the *Times Literary Supplement*.

'Curtain' is based on 'Die Vorhänge' by Bertolt Brecht.

for Liz

Contents

We hale the ship
as it leaves
the shore

our parting lives
more and more
given

the slip – the shore
is leaving
the ship

Dear Angelo

We are looking at the past. How clear it all is,
how detailed! The grain-lines in these oak planks
could be fresh from a print-shop's first pull
so distinct and candid they are: but touch them!

Baulks of timber, iron pulley-blocks, coils of rope
and piles of helmets and hammers litter the square.
They are demolishing one of the houses opposite.
What joy there is in the rush of falling rubble!

A boy trails hay through the breach in the sacristy wall
and horses are roped to a windlass not far
from where Sixtus and Fontana strolled a year ago
talking then of what is to happen now.

The obelisk is to be moved. It may take
900 men, 75 horses and 45 capstans,
but the obelisk – swaddled in reed matting,
boxed up in two-inch planking and plated with iron bars –

is to be plucked up by its roots like a leek.
Tree-length levers and wrist-thick rope
reeved and sheaved from a myriad pulleys
will free it from the muck of 1500 years.

Dandled from two oak towers, it will be tilted
onto a sled and hauled on rollers to its new site
in front of the new St Peter's: one in the eye
for the heathens of Heliopolis and Wittenberg!

The gold ball said to contain Caesar's ashes
has been removed from the point of the obelisk.
Pigafetta has examined it (there is *no* inscription)
and put its contents to the test of fire and water.

They are not human. Merely dust and earth
blown in through the holes left by the arrows
and musket-balls of the German mercenaries
who visited their mercies upon us in '27.

*

Today is the day. I resume at Summer's end
in the week of the Feast of the Exultation of the Cross.
May's procedure is reversed: the patient stone
to be winched aloft till poised above its astragals.

Dawn mass for the workmen, Sixtus blessing Fontana.
Crowds behind barriers, Cardinals dotting the roofs,
the visiting Duke of Luxembourg diverted to the square
to witness what Romans can do in Rome.

Swiss Guards patrol the mob bound to silence
(a rumoured gallows waits for the uninhibited)
so as the work can proceed to plan: a trumpet
sets the capstans turning, a bell stops them.

360 tons and 80 feet of ancient granite
carved, raised and honoured by the Egyptians
as the petrified seed of the God of the Sun
and shipped here by Caligula (ballasted by lentils)

now tremble aslant in September light.
Hooves clatter and slip on the cobbles, the ropes groan
and hold as the bell sounds one clear note and the ropes
groan louder, shivering out pizzicati like a giant harp.

The stone wavers mid-air, uncertain, held up by our eyes,
till one of us shouts, a repeated shout (what is he shouting?):
Water the ropes! Men running with buckets. *Water the ropes!*
The trumpet blasts the thing upright and the wedges go in.

*

A letter of stops and starts and the latest
a century back! Dear Angelo, good day to you!
I found this rolled up with writs crumbling into dust...
Yet your print faces the window bright as ever.

Proud to be Roman, I am prouder still
to have known you. Old now, I see our tottering life
suspended in the moment from its own frail towers:
what we do and what we make of what we do.

I listen again for that cry from the crowd
above the gossip and argument and rumour since.
There was no cry; a figment; no, it was 'a Genoan
with a garden on the river...' (O God of Detail!);

or, my favourite: 'an English mariner'. Why not?
Why not some lumpy sailor with a lumpy name –
Wegg or Waring, Higginbottom or Hodge –
or even a fugitive Milord on the spree...

Pigafetta says the notion of ropes saved by water
(and here's how I lose my cases) does not hold water.
Except if they were alight. I remember no fire.
Do I remember a shout? Sometimes I think it was me.

Mostly, though, it seems an exhalation of the crowd,
something risen from us like steam above cattle
as we watch not with envy, but knowledge.
The obelisk would not have stood without our watching.

Enough. I send these lines. I think of you
at your table sweeping the tiny sprigs and coils
of copper into an inky hand to toss them in the grate
where they flare green in the flames and are gone.

Albion

Four cricket-pitch lengths
of No. 16 copper wire

from the garden's oak
to the gable

feed in to the loft
where I sit

following the ships
through Atlantic static

The *Hood*'s
deckplate welds
lit like scars
Then she blew

The roses on Mater's nightdress
are asleep

with the treasury-bonds
in the sideboard

the stout-angled last
where Pater fixes our shoes

and his tin box
of sepia pin-ups

Curtain-up's gold
oak-leaves gleaming
from the caps in the stalls
Music drowns them

Each Sparks
has his own way

of operating
the sounder

each man's hand
as it's known

unique
as the set of his eyes

Bows-on the *Bismarck*
swells her haunches
Wind-slaps
of salt and sperm

A single star
stares through the skylight

then night
folds its wings

The dark
is fathoms deep

I listen
to men drown

Covering for Derek

The clash of lift-gates
and the motor's jerk and whine –
that'll be the post going up
or the rubbish coming down.

This is our knowledge: boiler-rooms,
the basement's flickery dark
as the fluorescent kicks in,
door-entry codes, the smell of keys...

If we're not so quick on the stairs
(our limp as seasonal as leaf-fall)
or seem to look after two properties
by being in neither,

remember – we were at this
when they were hauling granite at Giza
and clocking on at Babel.
It's been a long day.

We have lives of our own,
but not just yet. For now
we are staffage, local colour,
the distant Hodge only there for his hat...

Someone working late in Sotheby's
might look up as the fire-door bangs
and catch our Conduit Street shadow
crossing the chimney-pots...

Brazil

in memory of Mansour Khodr

I'd hardly slept: I listened as the clock
Ticked above my granite bed and pillow
  And I listened
To it change to tapping at my window.

Nearly dawn and someone tapping outside.
I sipped water, but then froze on the cup:
  Someone tapping
On my window, but my window's three floors up.

I looked outside and what I saw,
Stepping along the window-sill's weeds and dirt,
  Was a small bird
Wearing a Brazilian football shirt.

Fastidiously, on white-striped claws, it stepped inside,
Holding in the curve of its yellow beak
  A yellow book.
I took it and the bird began to speak.

A whirlwind of feathered words blew by me,
A thousand tongues at once, a million:
  That dainty bird
Had flown from Babel where they speak pure Brazilian.

I, though, was lost till the bird lapsed into English
With a nod at the book I held in my hand.
  'Take that to work.
The boys on Minus Four will help you understand.'

Then he was out on the sill, as if about to fly,
But spoke once more: 'Do me a favour. The least of things.
        Pull off my shirt.
It's awfully tight and I can't move my wings.'

*

As morning broke, I took the Red Core lift
Down as far as it goes, to Minus Three:
        The last level
Before the Opera House depths few dare see.

A closed metal door was covered with signs
And as I read, the lights crackled and dimmed.
        DO NOT ENTER
Said one; another, in pencil: *2 pints of skimmed.*

The door creaked open and I was clinging to a ladder,
Steel rungs disappearing into the dark.
        Minus Four stretched round me,
A vast gloom like midwinter in Hyde Park.

Nearby, a man in a suit was practising golf,
Sinking his putts, ball after shadowy ball.
        Who would think to look here
For the Chief Executive, Tony Hall?

Beyond him, the darkness suddenly split open
And flame and smoke contended on the noisy air.
        Two stokers, bright with sweat,
Beckoned me in to their Furnace Room lair.

Working in tandem, the two of them shovelled
Old costumes and sets into the furnace's roar;
        A mound of ballet-shoes;
The libretto of *Sophie's Choice* by Nicolas Maw.

Then they took the bird's gift, the book bound in yellow,
And I thought that too was for the flames, but I was wrong.
     They sang it in English
Waving their shovels in time with their song.

*

'Beneath the singers and dancers, the stage-hands and ushers,
Hear the song of the stokers, boys in a million,
     Bringers of light
Shovelling forever and singing in Brazilian.'

And I knew as they sang in the glare of the flames
I won't climb back up for a grand or a million.
     I'm one of them,
The boys waving shovels, singing in Brazilian.

Tower

Voluble builders from Akka
    in dromedary-skin boots
shoulder their hods, bending ladders
    of larch and spruce

past the carrel where I labour
    slow-parsing cuneiform!
I like their noise. I like the fact
    the building continues.

Citizens build the human hill
    on its own mine
and prove *What we build with our hands*
    is everlasting praise.

The ancient motto sanctifies
    the tablets and vellum,
the ruddy brick and stamped metal
    adorning each book-bay.

My work is theirs hallowed by time.
    Keeper of the Records!
My reading finger swells and splits
    like rotten papyrus.

*

Built ziggurat-style in massive curved steps,
the high structure generates its own clouds.
The top levels are streaked by damp and moss.
Cement is made from the silicious slime
Nubians bucket-dredge from the river
and bricks from whatever soil comes to hand.
The parts make up the whole: botched beginning,
disheartened abandonment, and ruin.

*

A mason hauled me to the top.
    Thick cirrus curled round us
and then the bright ball of the world
    fell away to the ground.

All roads led to our feet: each spoke
    with its bullock and cart.
Plumb sunlight caught a far river
    like the flat of a sword.

The mason was placing his fist
    in a crack in the wall.
'Just settling. Just settling...' he said.
    But now he's gone.

All night, wind blusters and buffets
    the creaky scaffolding;
library-scraps stuff my mattress
    and chide each move I make.

The crack is wider. In moonlight,
    brickwork and rock
dwindle. What we build with our hands
    is everlasting praise.

*

All the architects kneel
on trembling earth
to give thanks or beg forgiveness.

This is what they wanted
when young: to leave something
on the horizon. Done.

Hodge

for Alan Vaughan Williams

The more I think of Hodge
the more he comes to mind:
the prompt-corner ledge
curlicued with peel and rind;

his barn-door smile; his gloom;
the walk-in cupboard in the pit
he dubbed his dressing-room;
the way he always spat

and polished the leather
between sole and heel,
'Watch and learn, Oliver –
no bull like army bull...';

the way he was there and not there,
watching in the wings for hours,
then ghosting on; his flop of hair
as he bowed and gave flowers.

A Silent Letter

I like the fact
that the word 'aitch'
in many mouths
is aspirate,
the tongue bearing
letters-patent
all of its own.
We love excess.
Equally, though,
gaps can attract:
whatever's gone,
unforthcoming
or never was.
The middle name
you weren't given
shies from the noise
it makes itself,
a unicorn
deep in the wood,
and what you've lacked
in the last years
also mirrors
integrity
of a sort: warmth,
gentleness, tact.

Junction 13

Who moved his boots?
Who moved his soap?
Who moved his knife?

Who moved
what helped him
walk wash and eat?

Who stopped his clock?

*

I copied your key
noted the time
the light goes out

I measured the roof-space
oiled the chains link by link
steel soft on steel

I gauged your weight

*

I prefer not to talk
I do not expect you to talk
You cannot talk

Here's the pen
Make your mark
It might help you

It might not

*

He knows the cameras
He knows the slip-road set-down
the luggage-bay

He knows the one-mile walk
by verge and roundabout
to South Lake bridge

He knows the drop

Dactyl

From that swaying platform of planks
nailed to wrinkle-barked apple-boughs,
early fruit snapped from the branches
would volley across two gardens
to spatter and juice the Scout Hut
(our verdict on dib-dib-dobbers).

Old Spearman (known to us till then
by his porch skewed with milk bottles
and the late St Elmo's flicker
of TV on his net curtains)
once cursed us from the top garden,
his stick stuttering in rank grass.

In the lane, our wheezing football
(we had a pump but no adaptor)
wore new scars, gritted on leather
as we scuffed and flopped to Wembley:
too few for sides, so 3-and-in
smacking against a garage door.

Spread sun-crusted lane and gardens
as we were called to tea then bed.
Oliver was split, mockably,
by my mother's long and two shorts:
the low tail-off like our landing's
double step down to the bathroom.

The Meat-Safe

for Juliet

A shaded cupboard on a pantry shelf
at our Auntie Mabel's, a lozenge of coolness
fading into memory – peppermint, off-white, pale blue –
it had a perforated metal door (let it be zinc!)
through which, grail-like and numinous, the sacred
or profane is half-glimpsed half-imagined:

a tin of salmon, virulently pink,
the edging of its opened lid eager for blood,
or a stately bottle all-but-empty of milk,
its mouth shrouded by a diminutive doily,
a mantilla scorning the Cordoba sun...
Footsteps on a stone floor, the hush of the reliquary...

Out beyond the front-gate, buses and lorries
accelerate down Caerphilly Road into town.
Could the '12' I painted on the pillar
be both the house-number and my own age?
Dust and blossom tremble on the birdbath's water
as the past beeps its horn and overtakes.

In the living-room, I am forcing my sister to watch
The Man in the Iron Mask, the Sunday serial.
Plates cleared (our cabbage steaming the back-coals),
I chauffeur the trolley into the hallway's gloom
guided by the kitchen's ritual and response:
a teaspoon hitting the floor – 'Oooh, I've got dropsy!'

17 Melbourne Road

A room at the top of the street
preserving his life in sunlight
square-bottled brilliantine
a comb centre-parting a brush

work-boots on a page of the *Echo*
and the black jacket on its hanger
with the gold-threaded breast badge
of the South Wales Boxing Federation

Mondays my mother cleaned for him
the builder's mate and weekend referee
quiet and dependable as the man
sent ahead to hire a room for our Lord

still there as I close the door on emptiness
then and now looking back at our lodger
Mr Pudge caught in the honest '60s
small blue flowers pressed in a book

Jim Thomas

Was there some hint of Bogart about the precise
set of his mouth, clipping dialogue short,
or does the association come from the whites
he wore at work: the vest, rolled-up trousers
and sneakers fit for *The African Queen*...?

You left clothes, shoes and towel in a metal crate
swapped for a rubber tag gripping your wrist.
Echoes beckoned and bounced through the foot-bath.
Then light, the leap and smash – out, into and under
the blue world, bodies reborn as pale waverings...

Uncle Jim took our crates over a tiled counter
or dragged a red hose along the tiled floor,
water washing with water, the sweep of bristles...
Once, he was off ill – a leak of chlorine
bringing Passchendaele to the Empire Pool –

but was back days later, the inside man
for us boys grown wrinkled before our time...
Jim and Maisie lived in a sloping street
(Grangetown or Cogan) where his dry asides
roped and pegged tight the Big Top of her talk...

At his death, the City Temple remembered him
setting out, then clearing, the meeting chairs:
a servant as quietly true to his word
as the 'goodman' in the Gospel who furnished
a room for the Lord and was known by a sign:

'a man bearing a pitcher of water...'

Thomases Two

Born in adjacent years
on the same friable coastline

one found England
a bad smell

(but was published
in London)

worshipped the clarity
of the frozen stream

and took for gospel
the claw-marks of birds

the other marked his place in books
with rashers of bacon

lost the coating of his tongue
to a Vindaloo

(unpeeling it from his mouth
like a pink condom)

and sailed home from New York
in the Queen Elizabeth

the crew stacking his coffin
with whisky and wine

A Gazetteer of Welsh Waters

for Paul Henry

It was claimed today by a High Court silk
    the floods in Abertillery
    that closed the town dairy
were just the Welsh watering the milk

*

Withy and hide cast their miracle
    on Monnow's
    quick minnows
the shadow of a coracle

*

Down by the Dee in the altogether
    the Elders of Chirk
    are running berserk
Let us pray for a break in the weather

*

The Hamadryad's old porter
    waits in the ward
    on a sailor's last word
oceans shrunk to a sip *Water*

MVM

These lines
Commemorate
Marcus Valerius Martial
To Whom
All Rome
Was partial
He lived
On pith and zest
Died cursing
And leaves us blessed

Each word a brick
each line a street
your city now
stands on its own

the slow river
swinging her skirts
the noise and soot
softened by rain

*

Rugger-bugger roaring from the showers:
Big Jim's doffed his jockstrap.

*

Juvenal
and Johnson
walk together

as Latin nouns
land on the Thames
one by one.

The shadows
are different,
but not the sun.

*

Leaving the clap clinic,
he tried to walk tall:
would she still love him,
(genital) warts and all?

*

The editor's poems are never seen
in this small well-funded magazine.
Let's give credit where credit's due.
He won't publish himself. Would you?

*

She gave me the anorexic volume
on Richmond Bridge:
        her own.

It was all I could do
not to give it
        a dip.

*

My bed (I wish! my mattress rather):
        fucked;
my sagging crumb-filled armchair:
        fucked;
so no surprise about my back:
        fucked.

*

One of the things that gets to you
          about being poor
is pubic hairs – other people's pubic hairs
          on the bathroom floor.

*

          Marble-dust
          grizzles the furrows
          of a field in Kent;

          fallen columns
          are wound
          with longweed;

          this is good: ruins
          are the only home
          the gods now have.

*

Tom takes it up the arse with shouts of laughter,
          but cries, after.

Why? It's a copper-bottomed fact
          he just loves being fucked.

So which is it: shame before his lover
          or sadness it's over?

*

          Did this shy soprano
          mean to

          have her introitus
          seen to

in the under-gardener's
lean-to?

*

The sweet acres of woodland are all yours,
       ditto the Chippendale and Spode.
Yours is the only key to the cellars –
       those rare vintages rarely shared.

But your private bedroom's flushed full-length Klimt
       by speaking just the once
could tell what we all know (you alone don't):
       your wife is anyone's.

*

The slow pruner
picks a last grape.
Trajan's schooner
has cleared the Cape.
Gilding the stern,
her torches burn.

Martial, in Spain,
has earned this drink.
Outside, harsh rain;
inside, dried ink.
Built in a day,
these lines will stay.

*

Closer than swans to the Thames
or the lily to its pad
closer than vines to the elm
      is she to him
      the night they wed

Closer than waves to the shore
or swoop of swifts to the road
closer than rain in the air
        is he to her
        the night they wed

Closer than dew to the leaf
or blossom tipping each bud
closer than bees to the hive
        are both to love
        the night they wed

                    *

The cold Hippodrome crowd
        are all in white
except for Horatius
        whose cloak is black.

He smirches the white ranks:
        plebeian cloth;
senatorial silks;
        Nero's ermine.

All watch sudden snow lap
        the chariots.
When it clears, Horatius
        is cloaked in white.

This poem has won no prizes

This poem feels that giving prizes to poetry
is another way of not reading poetry.

This poem believes that literary prizes
are a part of PR, not literature.

This poem may contain traces of nuts.
It will not save your life.

This poem remembers when T.S. Eliot
was the name of a poet, not a prize.

This poem sleeps in its clothes.
It smells of old damp dog.

Please leave this poem
as you would wish to find it.

This poem crosses the garage forecourt,
the rainbows of spilt oil. Bye now.

A
Brief
Response
to Criticism

Having designed
and built
the Temple

for the statues
sitting in state
rather small

of Venus
and Roma
Hadrian

Venus
and Roma
might bump

invited
professional
comment

their heads
if they tried
to stand

Apollodorus
considered
the niches

Hadrian
had him
hanged

The Master

Trying yet again to tackle
one of the current bunch
(invidious etc. to name names)

I found myself thinking
Why am I reading *this*
when I could be reading James?

Democracy Comes to Iraq

I

The Colosseum's
understage corridors

are the width
of a lion's whiskers

The animals
cannot turn back

as we prod them
to the arena

II

In the innermost temple
of the inner ear
in the darkest corner
of the sanctum
      a whisper

The leader's lying to his people
was only a part
of his lying to himself
how could he
      not lie?

He supported the strong
against the weak
over-ruled the conciliators
and thousands helpless
      had to die

      How could he not?

Topping Out

Nubians bumped him up the ramp
with a modicum of pomp.
The Pharaoh clutched his vizier,
  dared not look down
and felt dizzier and dizzier.

The sun's one note was the note of a gong
as the Nine Vestals wobbled into song:
Brown and yellow the sands persist,
  Yellow and brown.
Our goats are dead but not much missed.

With dainty steps for one so large,
Nefertiti footed it from her barge
and processed through cheers and whistles,
  blithe as a lark.
The masons chinked their copper chisels.

Ithyphallic and hawk-headed,
roped off from the crowd they dreaded,
the Gods had a stand to themselves.
  Horus and Nark
loomed like carboys on pharmacy shelves.

The Pharaoh waved a golden trowel,
scattering consonant and vowel
on the mob prostrated below:
  Hereby declare...
Gifts of the Nile... Bloody good show...

The approving sun ended its descent
as torches lit us to palace and tent
and a flute's farewell tune
  thinned the night air.
The pyramid welcomed a timid moon.

Dowland

Congregations of cloud
    gull-grey gull-white
      flock and veer and crowd
               until night
          is a last bird calling
           in joy or pain
      above the rain falling
    gently the gently
falling rain

Morpheus

The kite of his breath
on its raggedy string

the mouth-cave's close smell
and mutters of sleep-speech

two yards of naked man
on a naked mattress

Oh oh oh Renfrew
Quiet now Hodge hush now

The jawline scuzz
the questionable nose

and stiff paintbrush swatch of hair
Hodge you looker you

Basilica ribs
troubled by plumbing

raw chipolata cock
and slow-mo balls

fretful legs and twitchy feet
where are you off to Hodge

you butcher's pin-up
where are you off to?

Didymus

Smears of Sumatran nard
    lengthened her spine
till impatient and hard
    I took what's mine

from one of the daughters
    stupid but rich
of Mrs Walters or Waters
    I forget which

    I forget which

Twice

for Chia Chi Wu

LILY: Stones in my hands and pebbles in my pockets

MAY: Stones in her hands

TOM: And pebbles in your pockets

LILY:}Stones in my hands...

MAY:}Stones in her hands

LILY: }and pebbles in my pockets

TOM: }And pebbles in your pockets

LILY: Stones in my hands and the river to my knees

MAY: To her thighs

TOM: To your waist

LILY: My dress water-weed

MAY: Stones in her hands

TOM: And in your pockets, pebbles

LILY: Once in the river and only once

MAY Not Liffey

TOM: Nor Tiber

MAY: Not Scamander

TOM: Nor Meander

LILY: Not never nor ever

TOM:} Not the Oos

LILY: } Not the Oos

MAY: } Not the Oos

LILY: Even when you're there, you're not there. Saying those things! But worse – the things you never say. Because you can't.

Dry stick. Your heart a desert. Your love – love! – sand. Your hour-glass mouth

MAY: Not Wandle

TOM: Nor Windle

LILY: Dindle-dandle

TOM: Asleep underwater and having to wake so as not to drown and waking at last to find yourself drowning in leaves, leaves falling over and over, ticking and tapping on your face

LILY: Not the Oos

MAY: That mouth on him like a gash. Like someone slashed his face. I told her. It's a cruel mouth. Never mind love you and leave you – it'll be fuck you and leave you. Over and over. If you're lucky

LILY: Out into the Sound, the castle black above us

TOM: And the boat's wake behind, white on blue

LILY: Walking apart on our island

TOM: Kept company by shingle

LILY: The shush of shingle

TOM: Taking our small flat stones back to the jetty

LILY: And then skimming

TOM: Skimming them further and further

LILY: Further and further out

TOM: Four!

LILY: Five!

TOM: Six!

LILY: Dapping and skipping

TOM: Far flicks of white as they kiss the sea

LILY: Oh! Far flicks of white

TOM: As they kiss the sea

LILY: Out

TOM: Out

LILY: Into the Sound

MAY: Some Greek or Roman. Some old piece of toga. Demos...
Demos... Some Greek or other. An orator with a stutter taming
his own stammer. Walking the beach with a handful of pebbles
in his mouth. Out-talking the waves. His clapped-out tongue like
the clapper of a bell. Then he comes to the – what is it? – the
Senate and knocks them dead. Demosthenes!

TOM: You don't say.

LILY: Things don't finish. Things aren't over. How handy for you
if they were. They aren't. What you said goes on being said, what
you did goes on being done

MAY: Over and over. I told her

LILY: You think it isn't. Just like you think you're not here. Well,
you were never there even when you were there, and now you
say you're not here, well, bad penny, here you are

MAY: Back then we thought – if we bothered then with that,
thinking – we walked as if through nothing. Whereas, at the
least, I said, there was air

LILY: We walked through air

TOM: And now we walk through water

MAY: Over and over

LILY: The river over

MAY: Not the river over

LILY: The river over

MAY: } Not the river over

TOM:} Not the river over

LILY: The river over

Nim

Let the two of you
randomly divide
a pile of stones
into any number
of heaps
then each
in turn

remove
from a single heap
one or more
or all
of the stones

and whoever takes
the last stone
or stones

wins

Marienbad

That year I forget if we
used poker-chips or not

but coming in
out of mist

and topiary
bare arms on baize

framed the usual game
where she and I

had to take
as many or as few

as seemed fit and
whoever picked up last

lost

Goethe Twice

I

Laying down your arms
for the nervy qualms
of a Quisling
and little girl grizzling
will neither console
nor set you free.

Might feeds its fill
on our ill-will
and thereby thrives.
Cap-in-hand lives
dream of rebellion
but bend the knee.

II

The mountain-peaks
hold their breath
and nothing speaks
on earth.
The wood is a nest
of sleeping birds,
a prayer beyond words:
rest now, rest.

Morgenstern Ditto

I

Morgenstern took to aping the animal order
Savile Row kitting him out in feather or fur

You'd catch him with your Zeiß – from far below –
in the crest of an oak and the guise of a crow

or up some alp in shaggy-dog costume
and at his neck a keg of schnapps or rum

He left us as a stork (by then he'd flipped)
hanging from a Zeppelin bound for Egypt

II

The sheep blinked up at me as if seeing
        its very first human being

and put me under – surfacing from sleep
        I saw my very first sheep

Take Three

Day's watermark is the moon's face
    faint unsleeping
with all the roofs of Chandos Place
    in her keeping

*

Though the dead spit of Terence Stamp
    he's a poodle-faker
nothing but shrapnel for this tramp
    on Long Acre

*

Mayfair drove them mad then madder
    with snow then sleet
two Poles carrying a ladder
    down Pollen Street

The Austen Machine

What must be at last
Had better be soon
From the flaring match
To the waning moon

What we love the most
Will drive us insane
Every seed of hope
Bears a crop of pain

Our heydays of lust
Sicken after noon
What must be at last
Had better be soon

Each gleaner a ghost
On the fading loam
The swathes of the past
Are harvested home

What must be at last
Had better be soon
Ardent brides in March
Break their vows by June

Sung slowly or fast
It's the same old tune
What must be at last
Had better be soon

Keats

Moonlight
on the shelves

and the spines
look solemn

All those words
but the only sound

is the tongue
of the library cat

busy at a saucer
of cold sweet water

18 Geo. II, c. 27

Every Person or Persons
who shall by Day or Night feloniously steal

any Linen, Fustian, Callico, Cotton, Cloth
or Cloth worked, woven, or made of any Cotton
or Linen Yarn, mixed, or any Thread, Linen or Cotton Yarn,
Linen or Cotton Tape, Incle, Filleting, Laces, or any other
Linen, Fustian, or Cotton Goods or Wares whatsoever

laid, placed, or exposed to be printed,
whitened, bowked, bleached, or dryed

in any whitening or bleaching Croft,
Lands, Fields, or Grounds,
Bowking-house, Drying-house, Printing-house
or other Building, Ground, or Place

made use of by any Callico Printer,
Whitster, Crofter, Bowker, or Bleacher

for Printing, Whitening, Bowking,
Bleaching, or Drying of the same

to the Value of ten Shillings

or who shall aid or assist
or shall wilfully or maliciously
hire or procure any other Person or Persons
to commit any such Offence

or who shall buy or receive
any such Goods or Wares so stolen,
knowing the same to be stolen as aforesaid

shall on conviction be deemed
guilty of Felony
without Benefit of Clergy

and be punished with Death.

Slip

In writing the word Fräulein
instead of putting the umlaut
above the a
he had put it above the u

The more she looked
at that double-stroke
above the open letter
the more Freudian it grew

The View from the Border

How odd to prefer the Germans
      to the French
the mere thought of all those Hermans
      makes me blench

How strange to navigate the Rhine
      not the Loire
hoisting the flags of *Ich* and *mich* and *mein*
      above *Moi*

Denigrating a whole nation
      how remiss
unless we grant them one consolation
      They're not Swiss

Quba

It was one of the old up-country plantations –
a room with tiger-skins yawning on the floor,
orchids in an ice-bucket of water
and the quinine-slow nodding of his skull
as the gas-jets wobbled yellow and blue.

He'd clinched the deal as the century turned –
a printing-press using native labour ('Peanuts!')
for a trial-run of stamps for the new set-up.
He passed me a book, rum-sticky fingers
stubbing an entry: *For England, see Wales.*

Stamps of waterfalls, stamps of breeds of sheep,
stamps of tractors, stamps of beer, stamps of coal,
stamps of the universe seen from the Bay,
stamps of stamps. 'The world perforated! Gummed!'
His bonobo shrieked and whooped on its chain.

'And I played long. I kept all the misprints.
Twenty years on, I watched the market twitch.
A scarlet daffodil held the front page.
Snowdonia (upside down) went to Dubai.
Tim Jones (Tom) – for millions. I had it made.'

He up-ended the bottle and the flames
in his dead pupils doubled and tripled.
'How do you improve on imperfection?
I made a world. Now, I drink it away.'
The ape held out a palm. 'OooOooOooOoo!'

Seven Types of Meat

A time of floods and me wanting to kill someone
(not just anyone – a certain woman – but no names...)
when we met by chance and I was in your room

ceiling and windows dilated by light
children passing outside *en arlequinade*
and your heron-stepping self emphasised

by a mask lozenged with violet and red
above a gorget or beak projecting
your high-tension intellectual twitter

of complaint about an electric nail-buffer
(its covetable dentist-drill pulley-mechanism
with an anglepoise awkwardness to match your own)

not doing the job as well as an emery board
That's the way of it, I'd said, the older the form
and the more you put into it the better the result

then wondering (worrying) I was making a criticism
but that's all water over the bridge
the three of us waded to wait for bus or boat

your scrunch-haired girlfriend hugging me
and I unsure of who was going and who staying
till I broached the matter of my case left on the bed

its mound of twenties with torn-off corners...

Old Usher

for Farès Moussa

I have
shouted Lights! in the foyer as the show begins

I have
opened and closed a million doors
Push and Pull stamping my palms

I have
woken with Good Evening on my lips

I have
ROH in moles over my left nipple

I have
Tchaikovsky as a heart-beat

I have
told ten thousand bladders
It's down the slope and on the right

I have
stood at the bottom of Floral Hall stairs
with Peter Bramley at the top
tapping the metal hand-rail with his ring
to annoy me

I have
bent my head to complaints about the row in front
the big hair-do, the change-jingler, those who snore or smell

I have
turned a blind eye, a deaf ear, and a stopped nostril

I have
opened and closed a million doors
Push and Pull stamping my palms

I have
waited in the wings to present flowers
cygnets wafting past me in a crush of tutus
each back tight with the cordage of muscle

I have
sold ices with Susie Boyle

I have
passed the black-and-white monitor at Stage Door
and felt proud to see Haitink in the pit
a bottled homunculus preserved in music

I have
opened my locker on a vista of dirty shirts

I have
killed a moth for Monica Mason
It wants to *settle* on me!
she who once danced her death in the *Rite*
now frightened of millimetres of flutter

I have
Tchaikovsky as a heart-beat

I have
bassoons and strings planned for my last-act death
the weightless *pas-de-chat*
lifting me out of this ninth life
into the proscenium's eternal gold

I have
perfected my farewell
a final turning-out of the pockets

as I rise and vanish into air
swirling with the confetti of ticket-stubs

I have
shouted Lights! as the show begins

I have

Curtain

On the main curtain paint Picasso's
contentious dove of peace. Behind it
stretch out wires on which I want
two light fluttery curtains
to foam together like waves
so that a woman giving out leaflets
or Galileo recanting can be whisked from view.
As the repertoire changes, so these curtains
will be rough linen or silk,
red leather or white, whichever suits.
But don't make them too dark –
scene by scene they'll be the screen
for projected captions moving
the cliff-hanger on from catharsis
to thought. And make them such a length
as teases – conceal to reveal.
Let those settling in the stalls and gods
realise this bustle of preparation
is meant for them: the tin moon
climbing the sky and the roof of planks
pushed into place are glimpsed
and then gone. Let the audience come to see
that you busy yourselves not with magic
my friends, but work.